The first two photos in this book represent the basis for the following set, all of which were created by multiple algorithms to produce more abstract views. This post-processing includes using apps available commercially as well as my own programs. For those reminiscing about the days when photographs and art in general required the use of human control of algorithms consisting of canvas, pencils, and brushes, please know that all of the processes required to make these drawings required human physical and mental control of hands and brains and were not limited to hardware and software computational components.

Light
On
Water

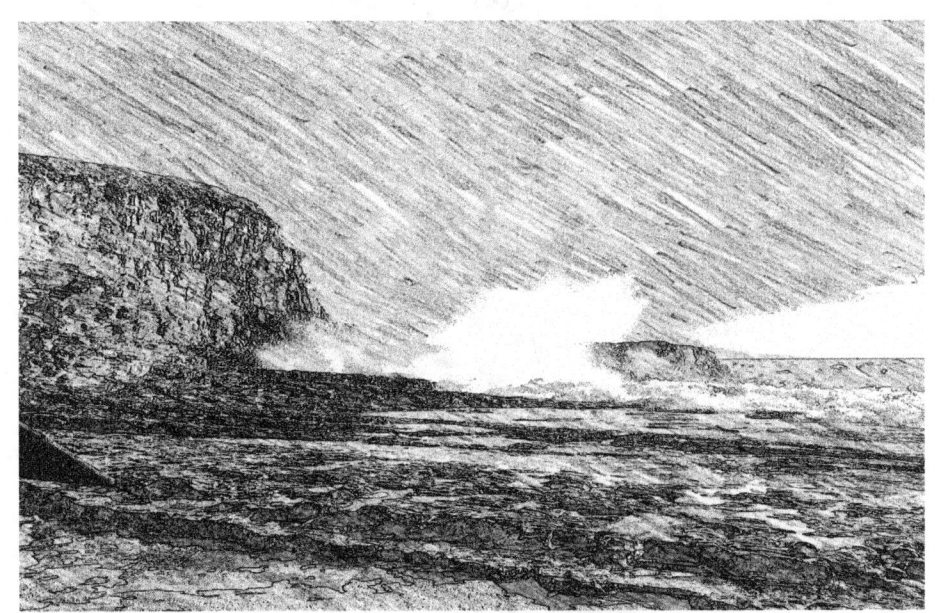

Photographs
By
David Cope

Light on Water
Photographs by David Cope

Epoc Books
Printed in the United States of America
© David Cope 2016
All Rights Reserved.
Published 2016.

This book is dedicated to my wife, sons, and grandchildren, Zoe, Tess, Gavin, and Ethan whose excitement for everyday things never ceases to amaze me. And to those older kids like me who believe in those children.

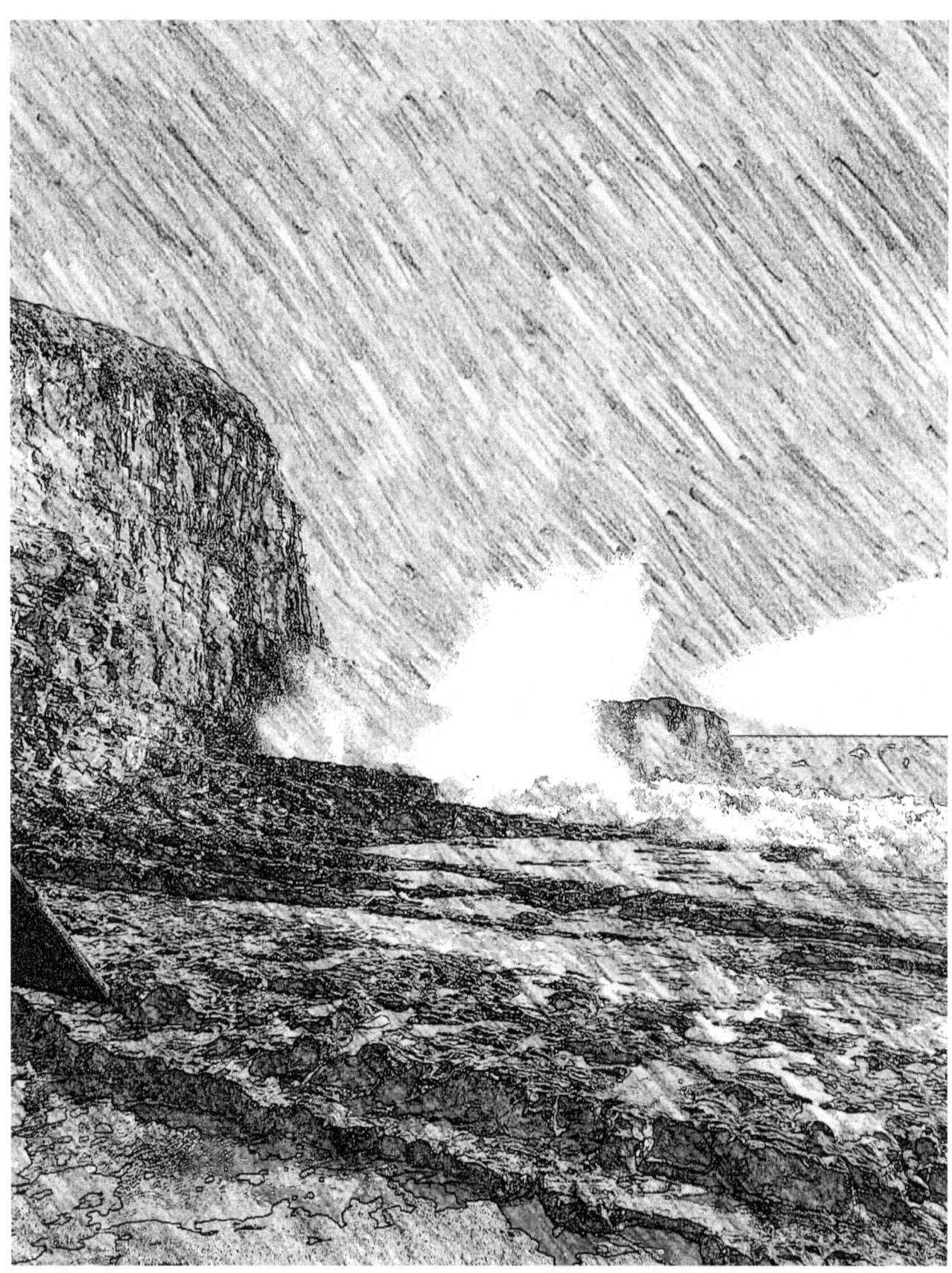

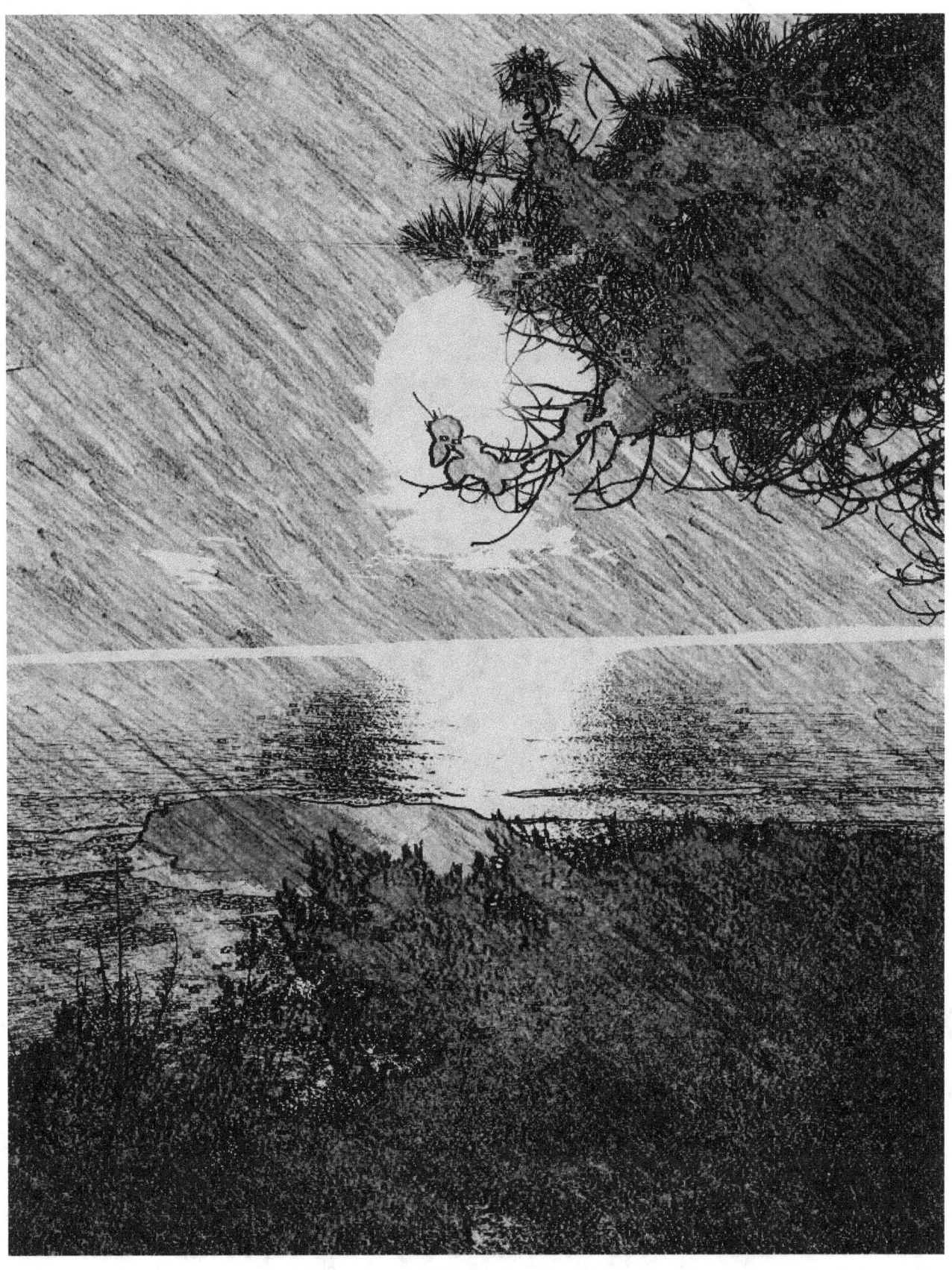

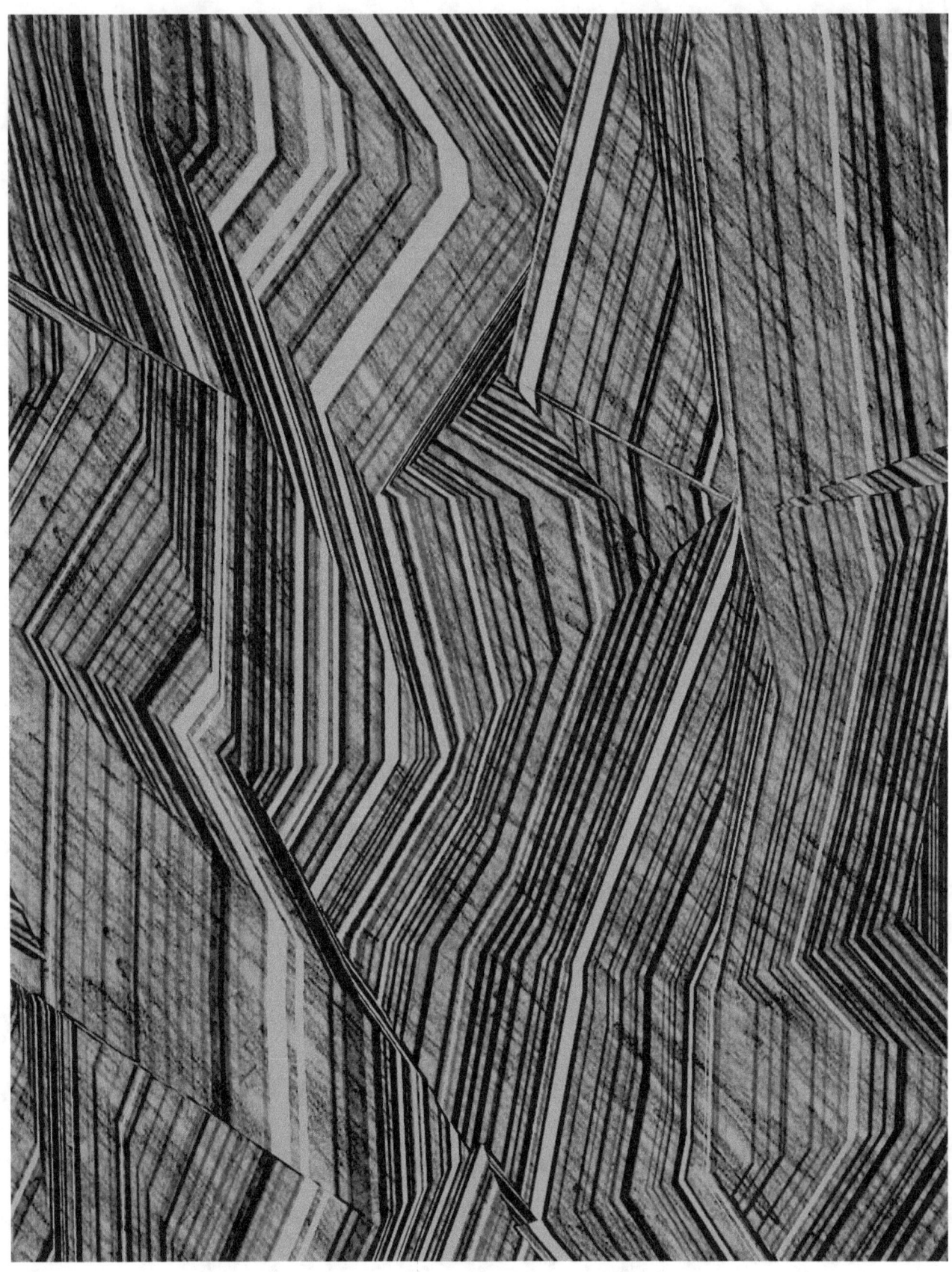

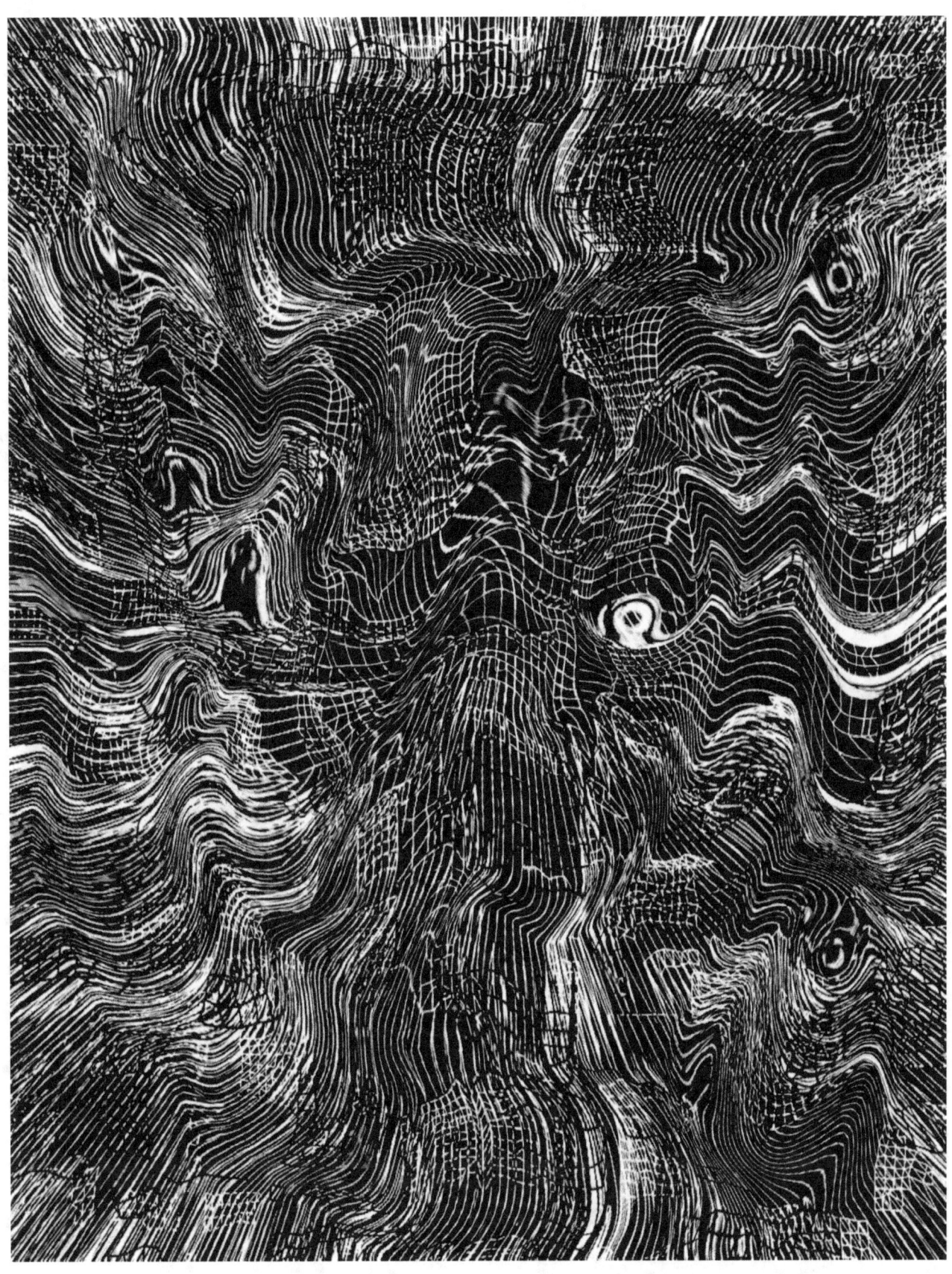

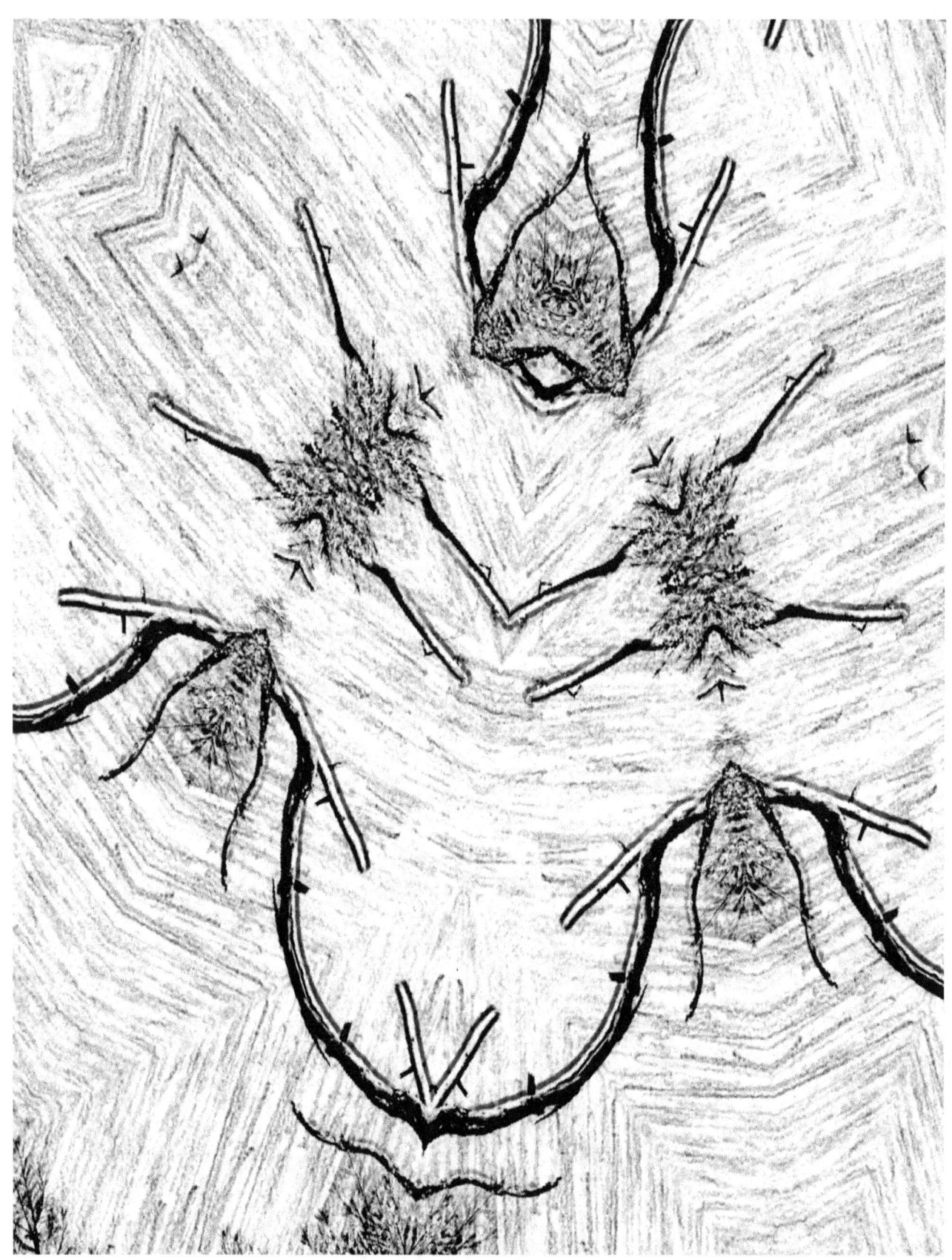

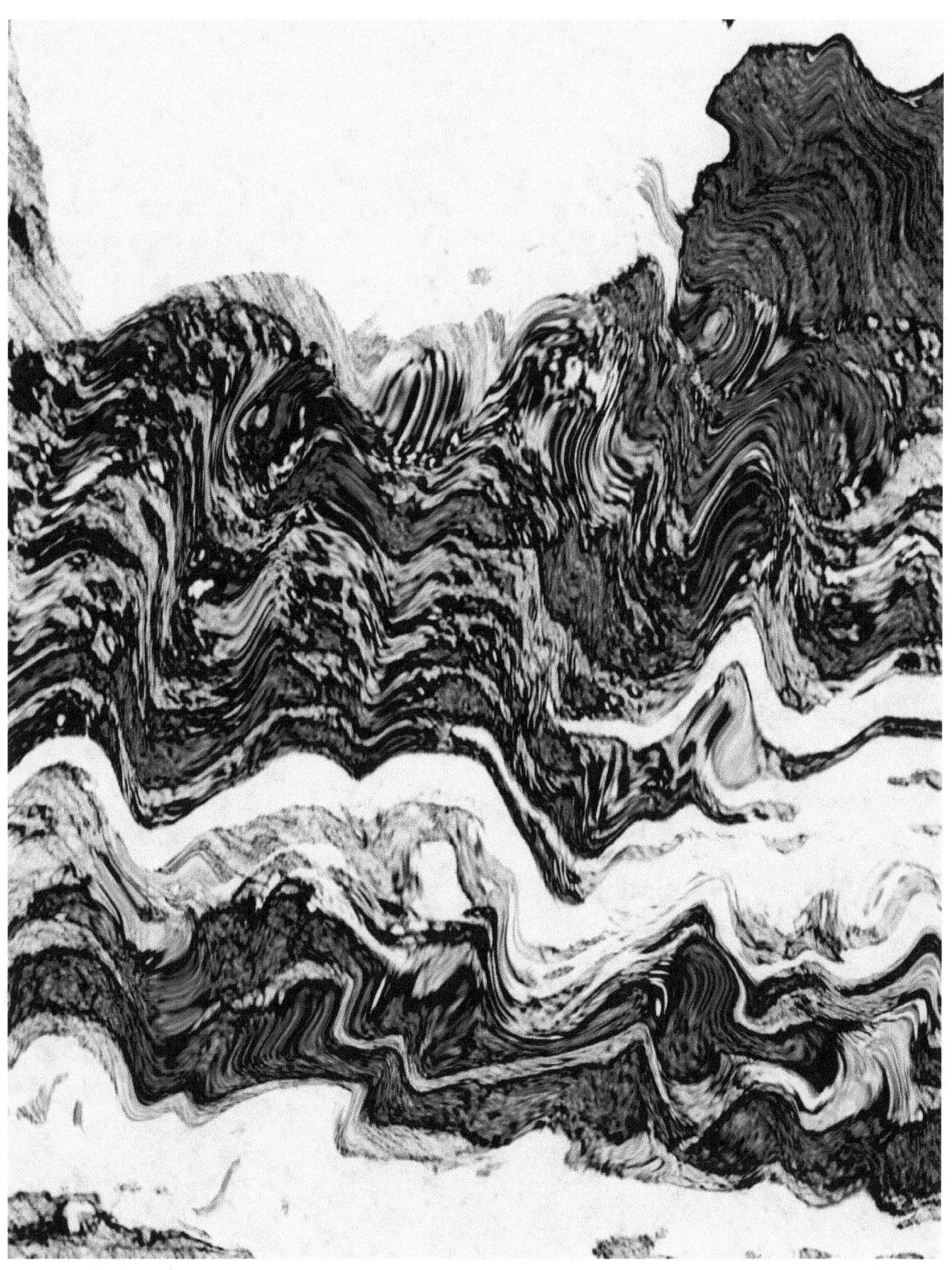

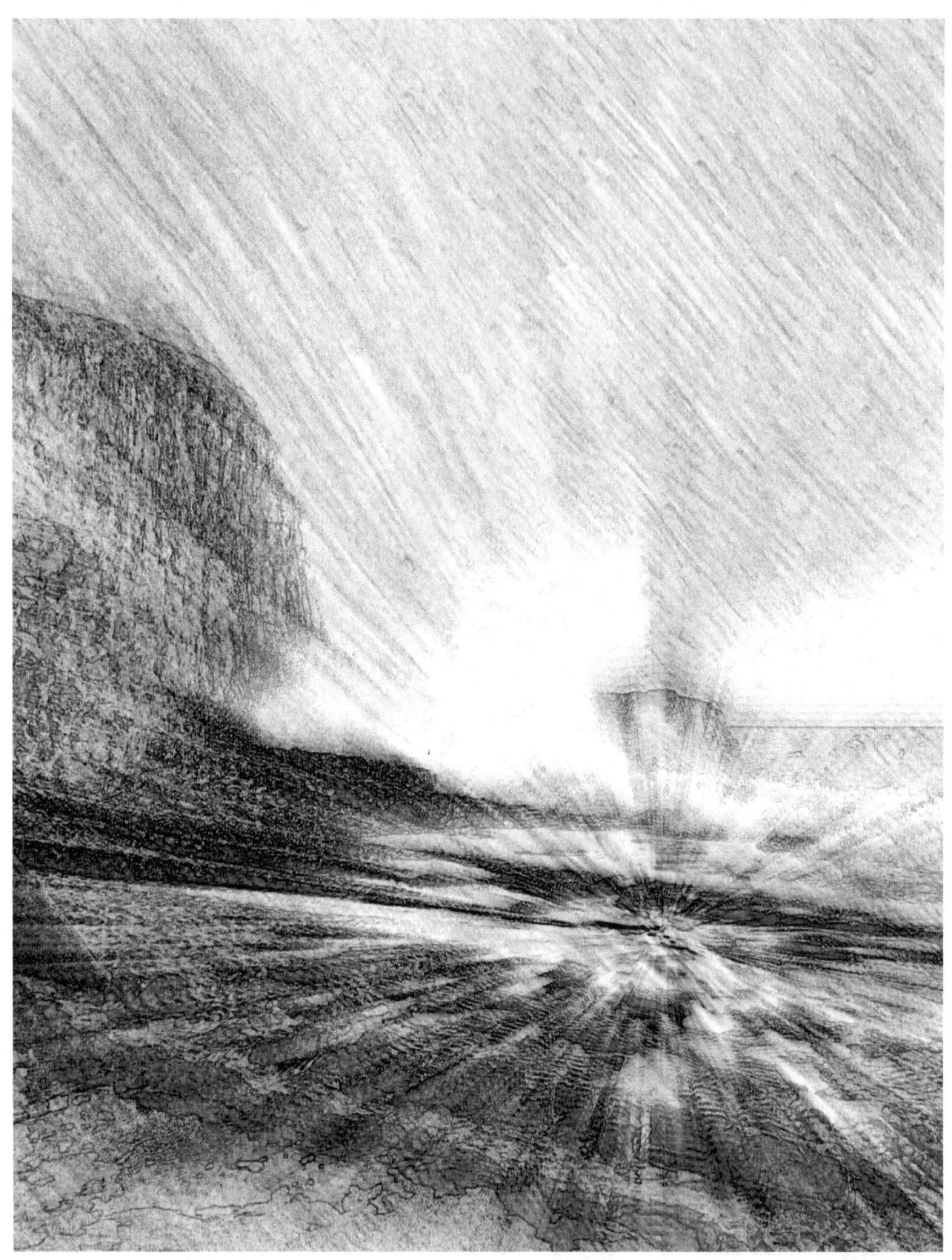

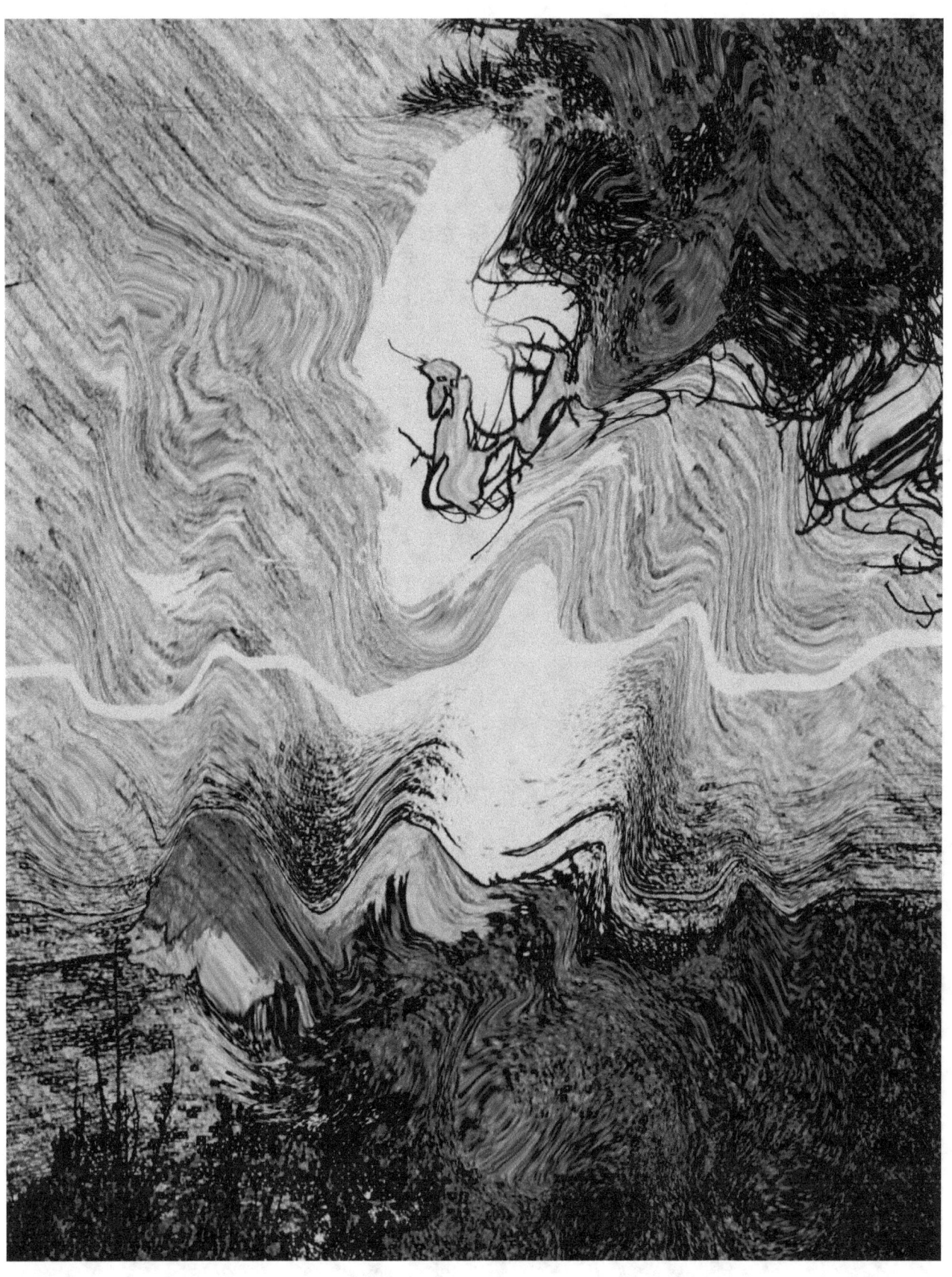

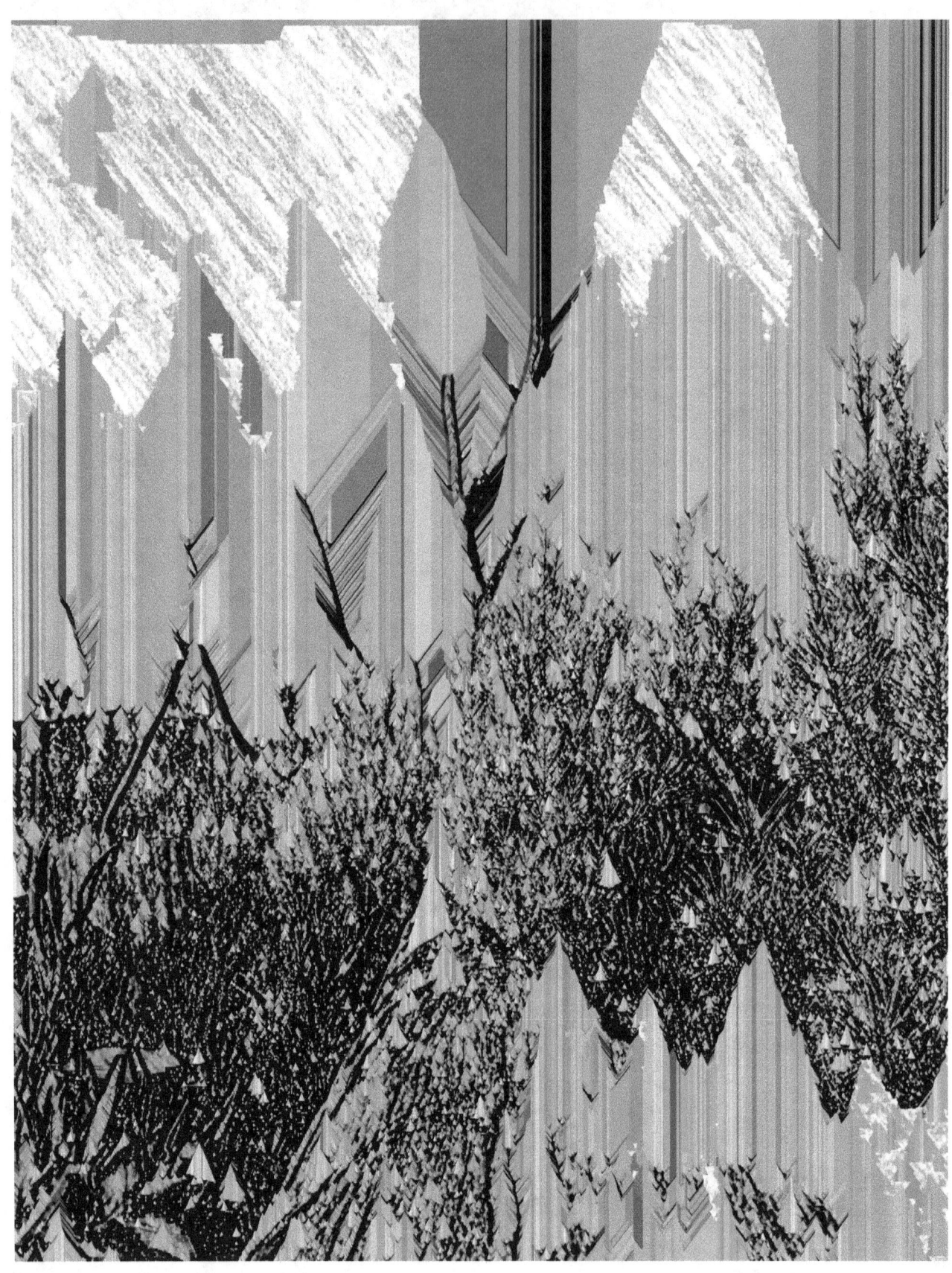

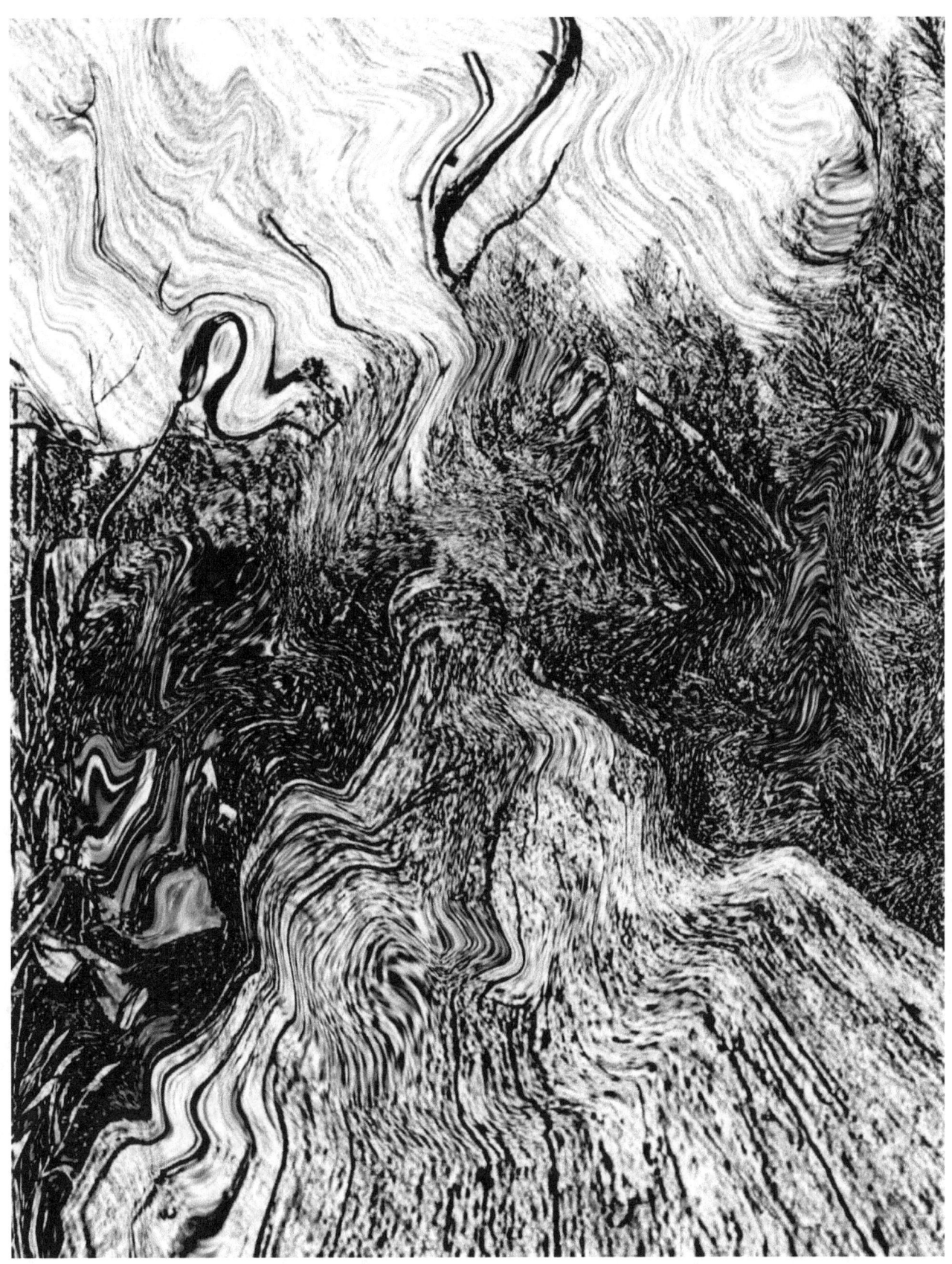

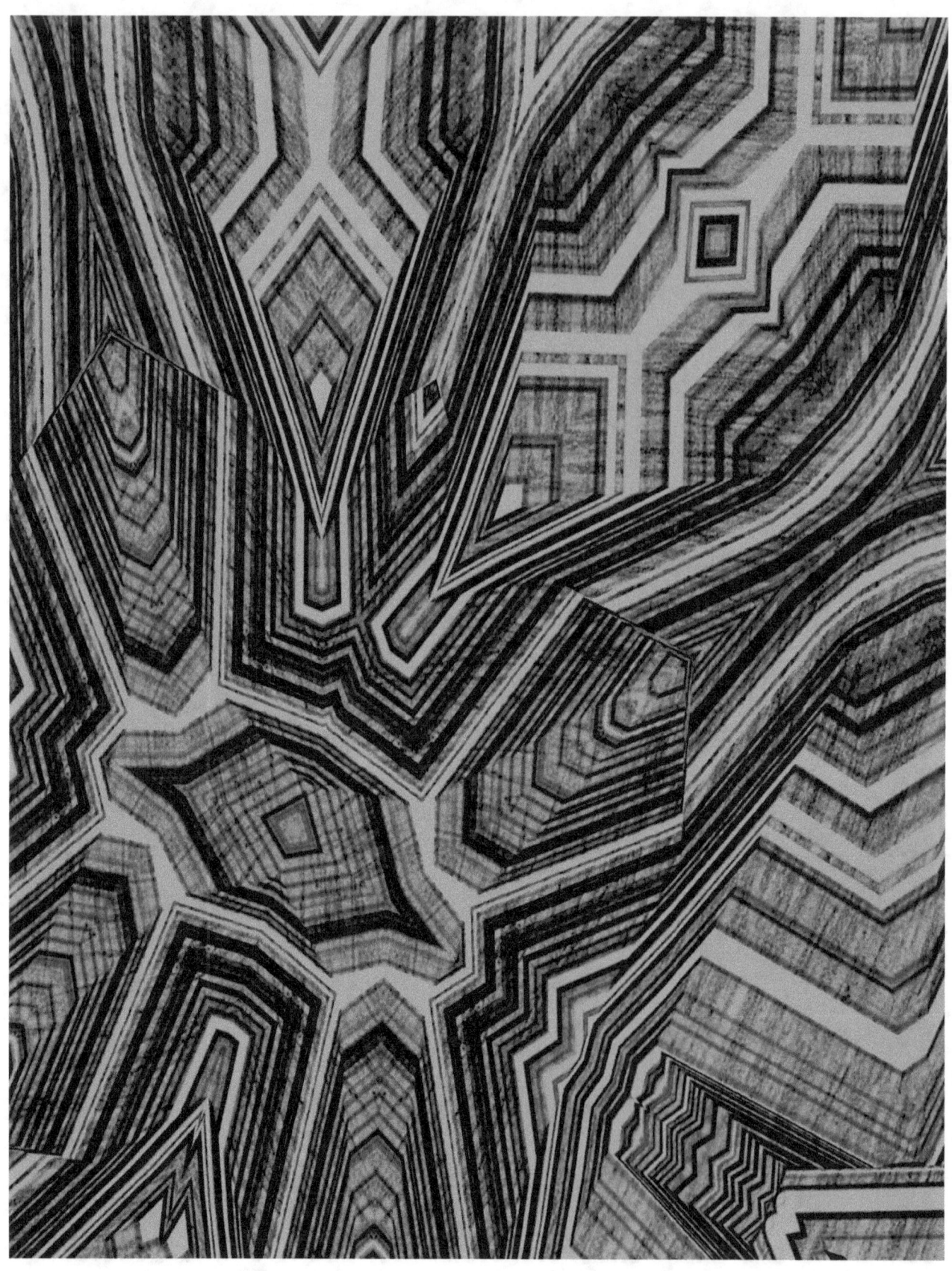

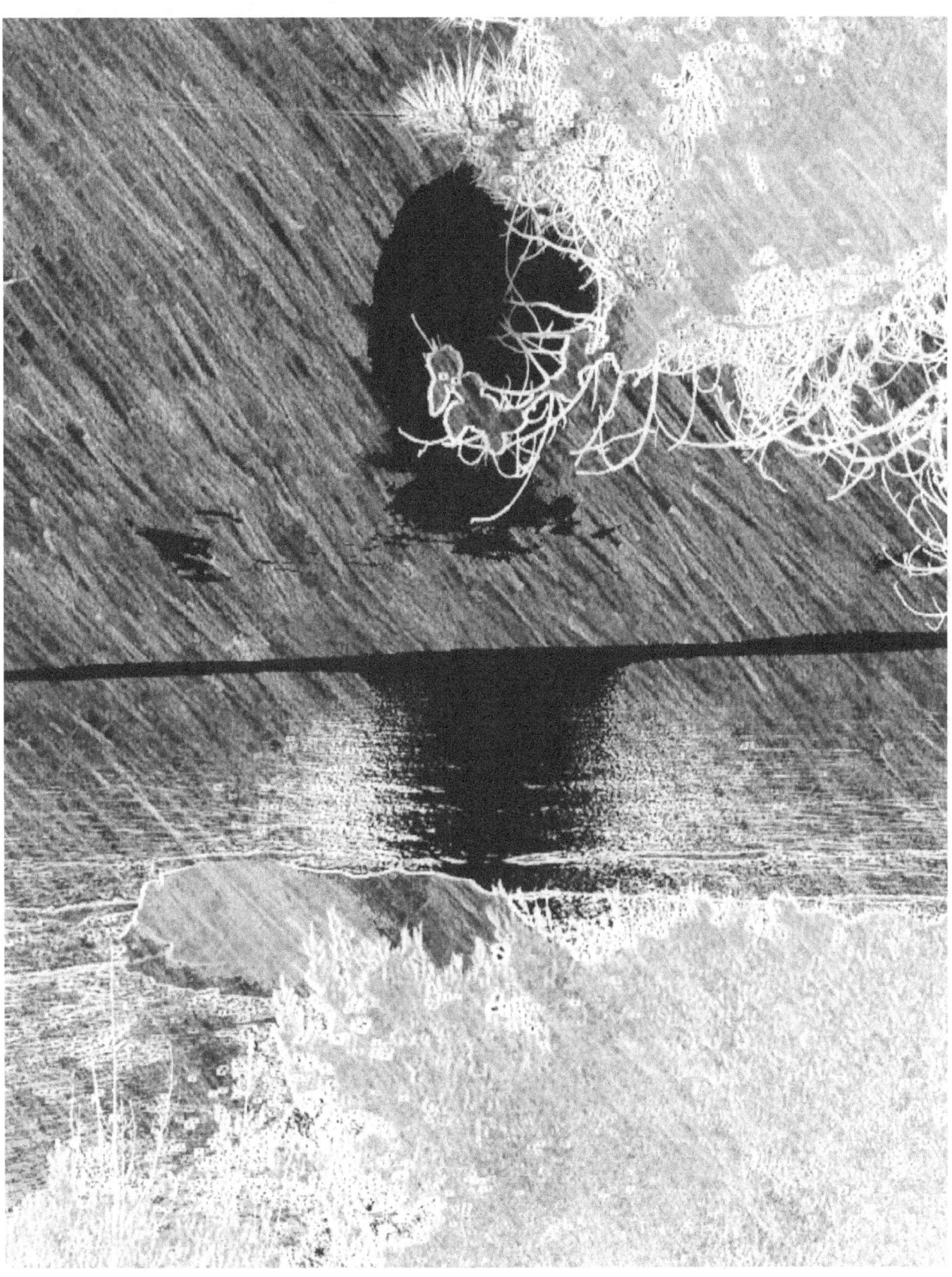

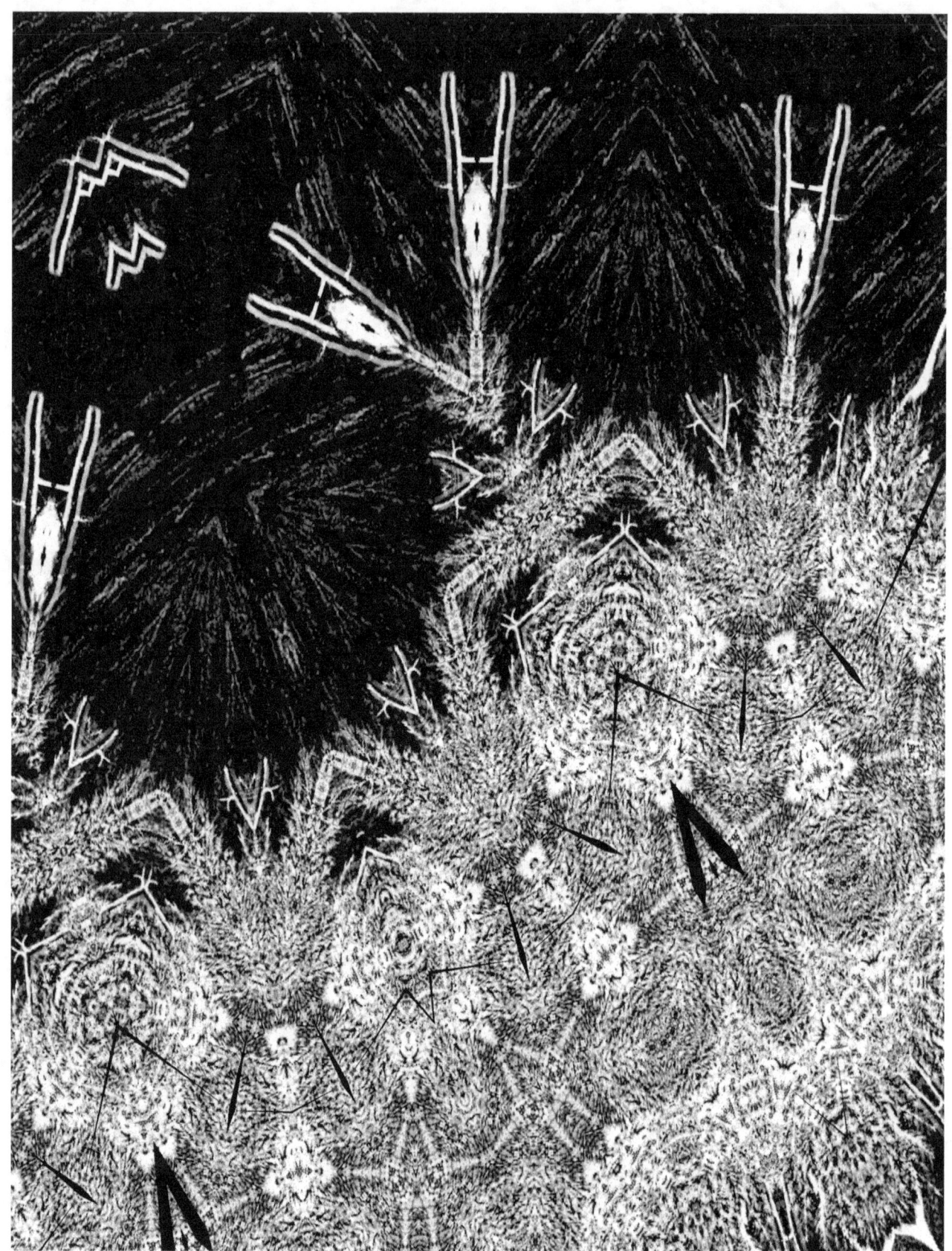

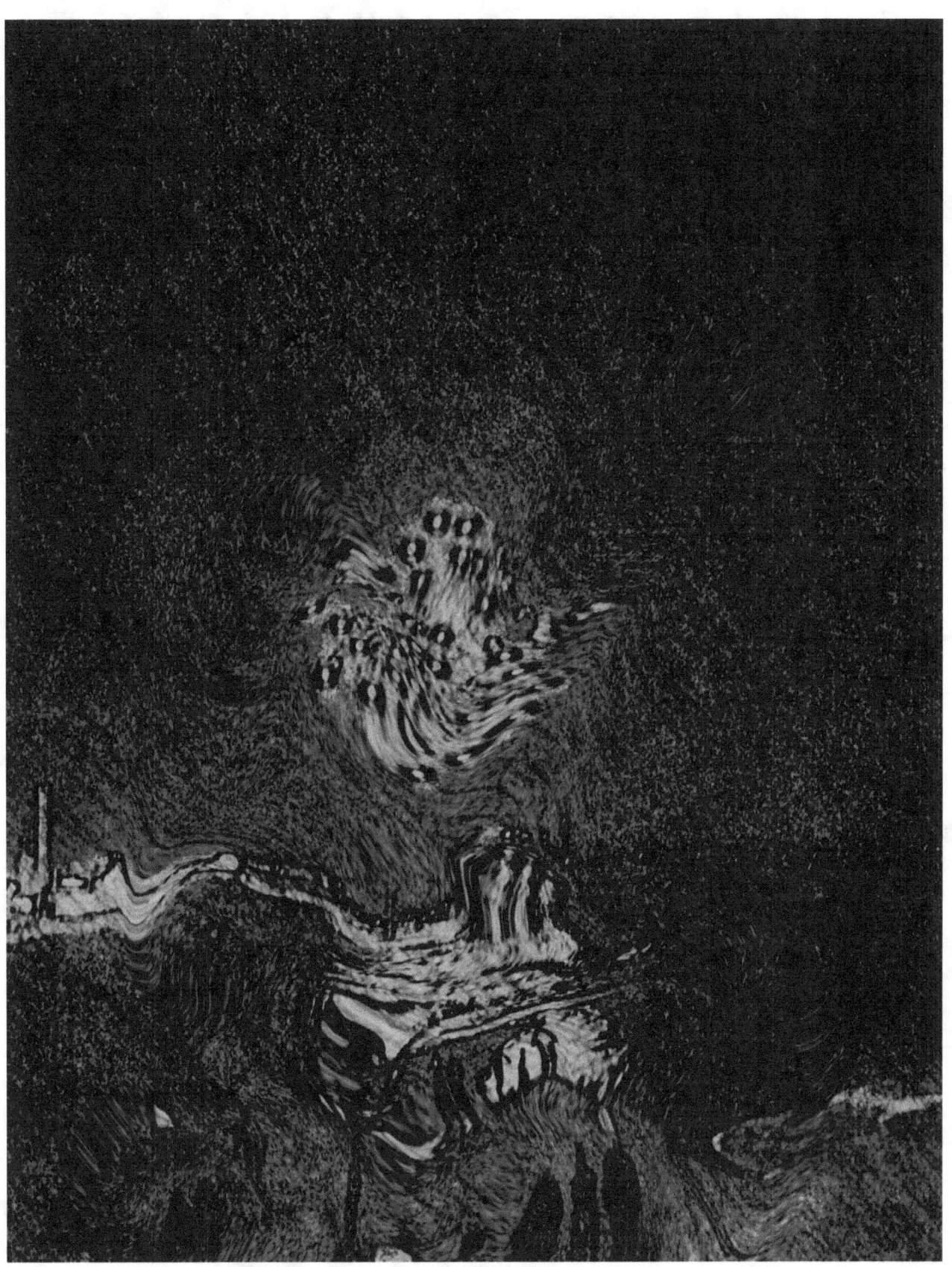

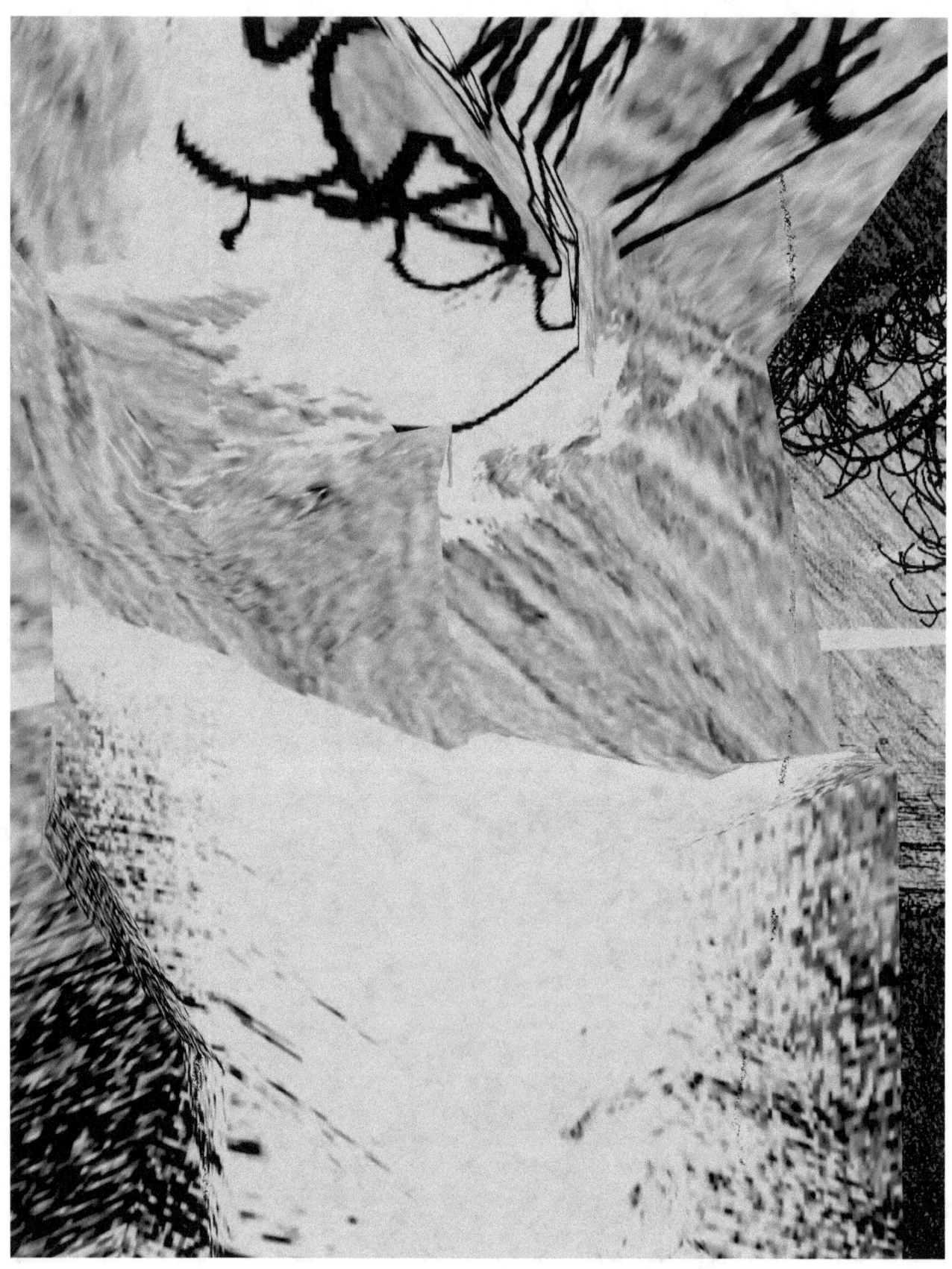

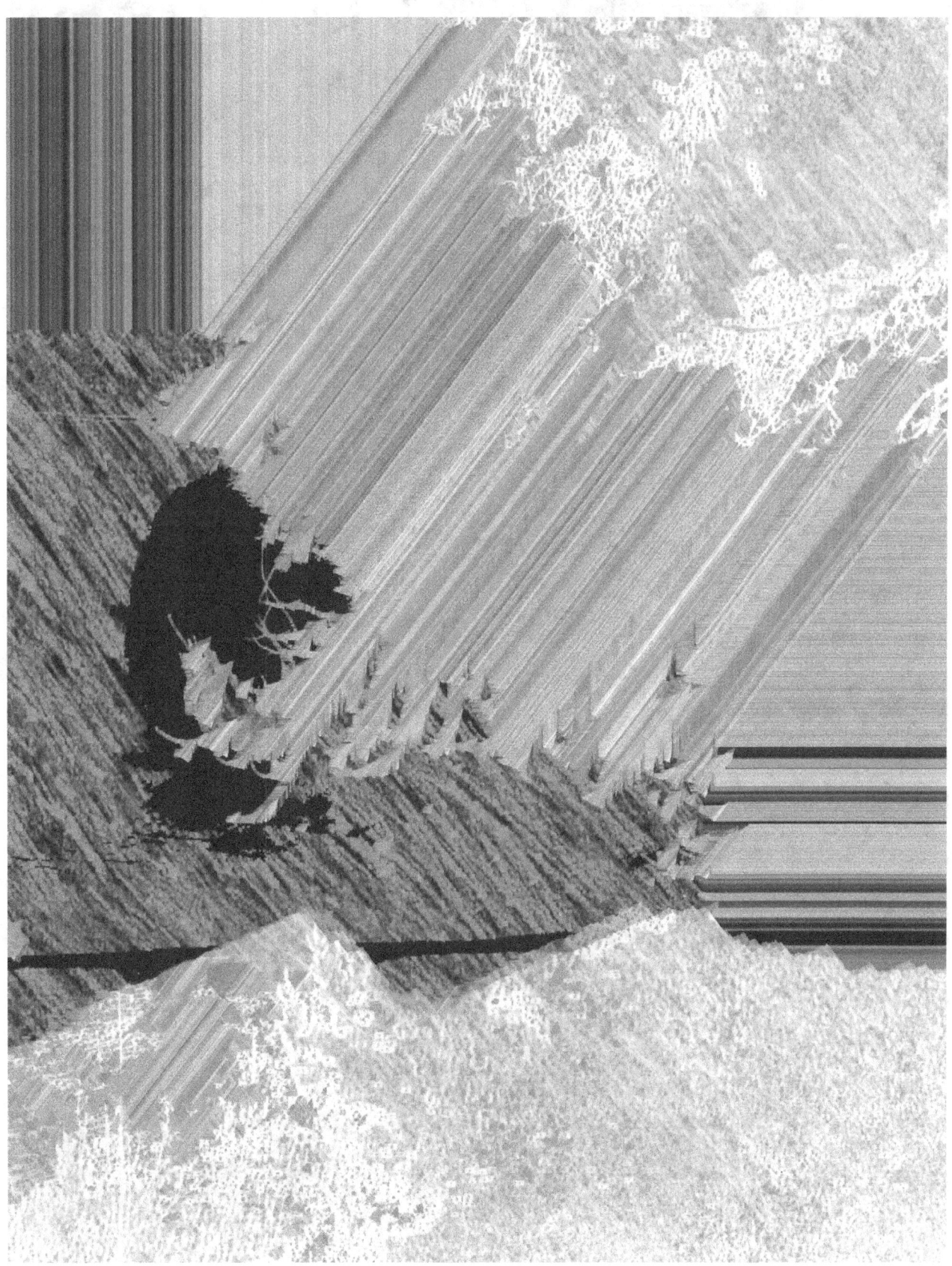

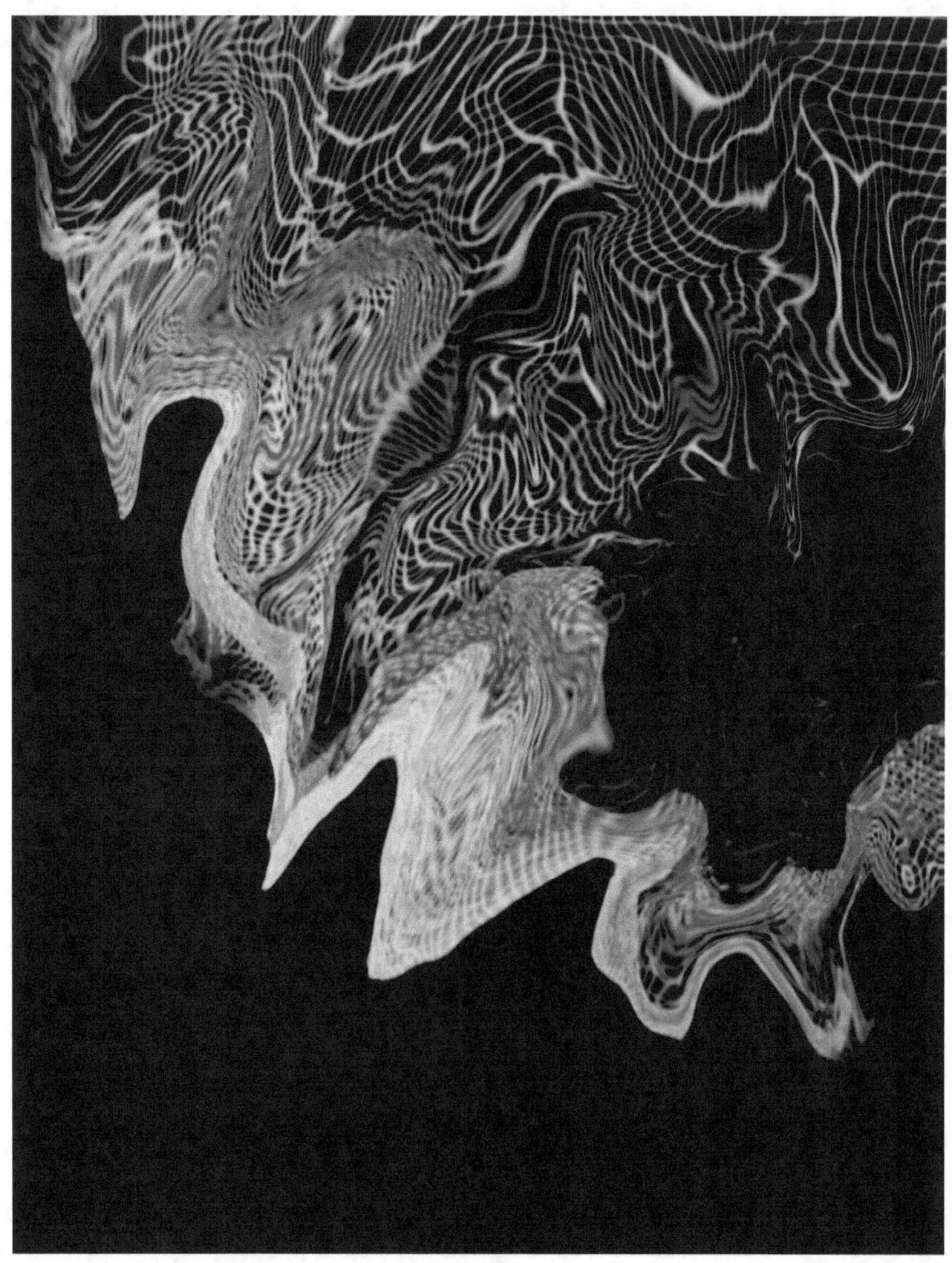

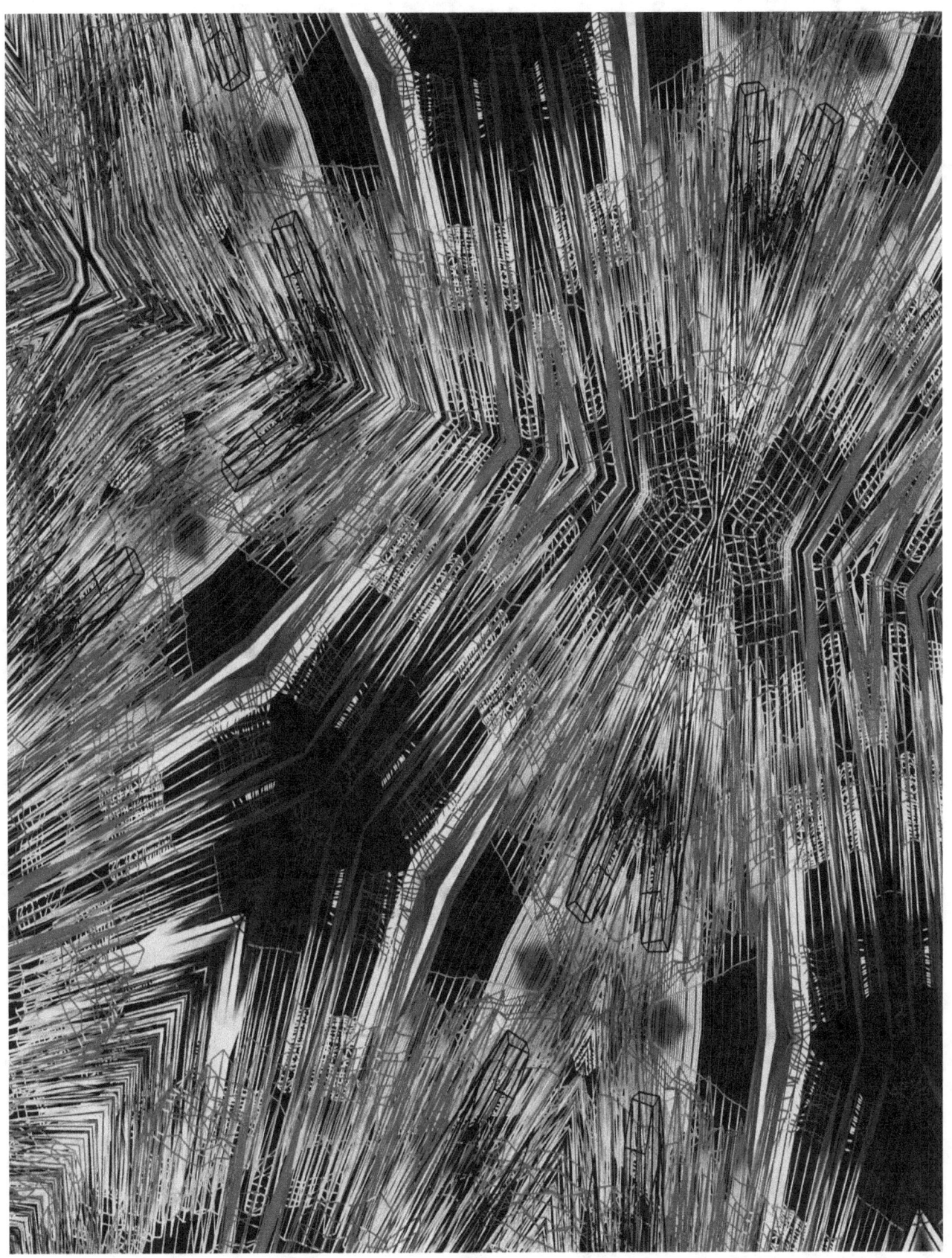

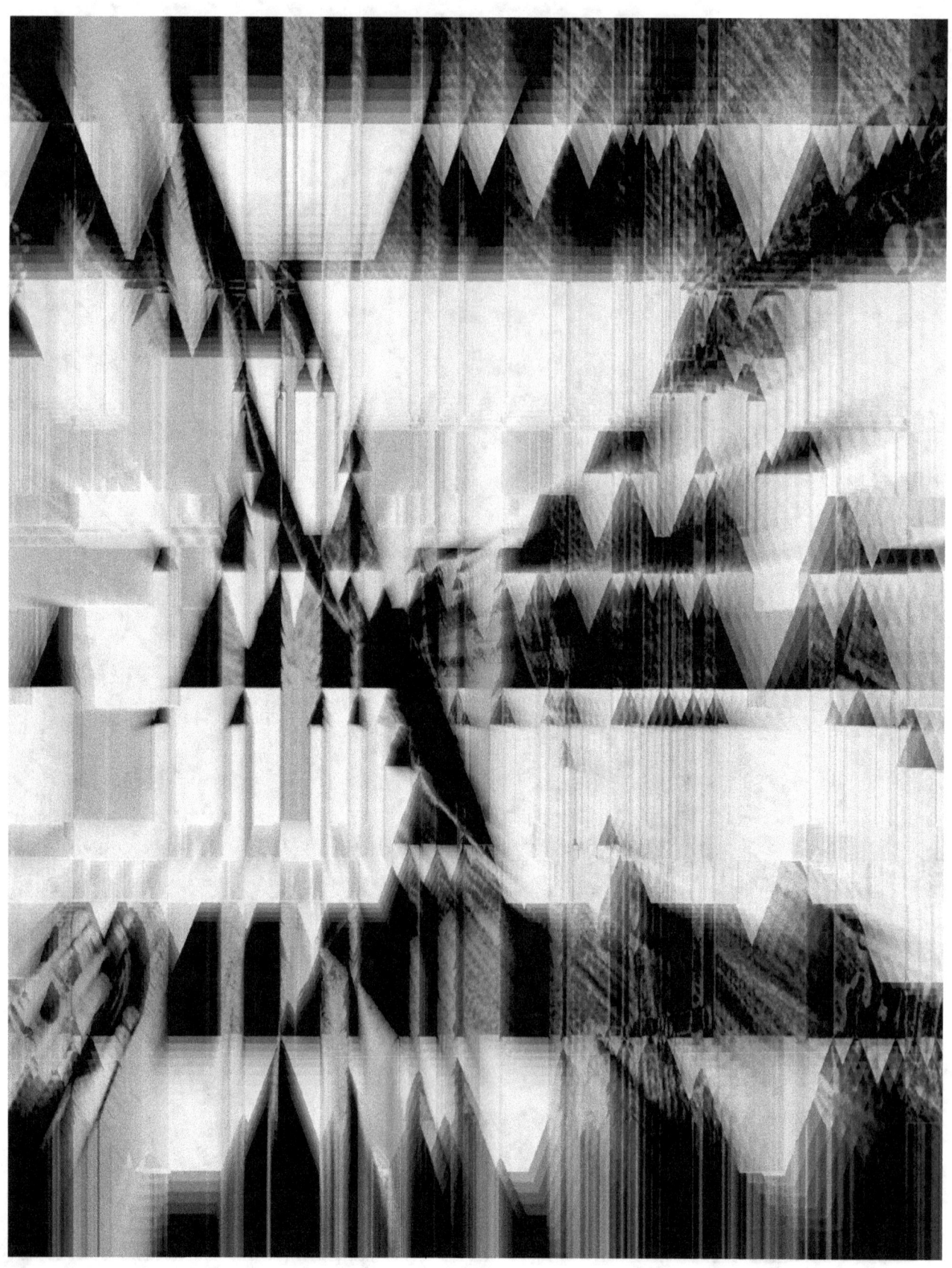

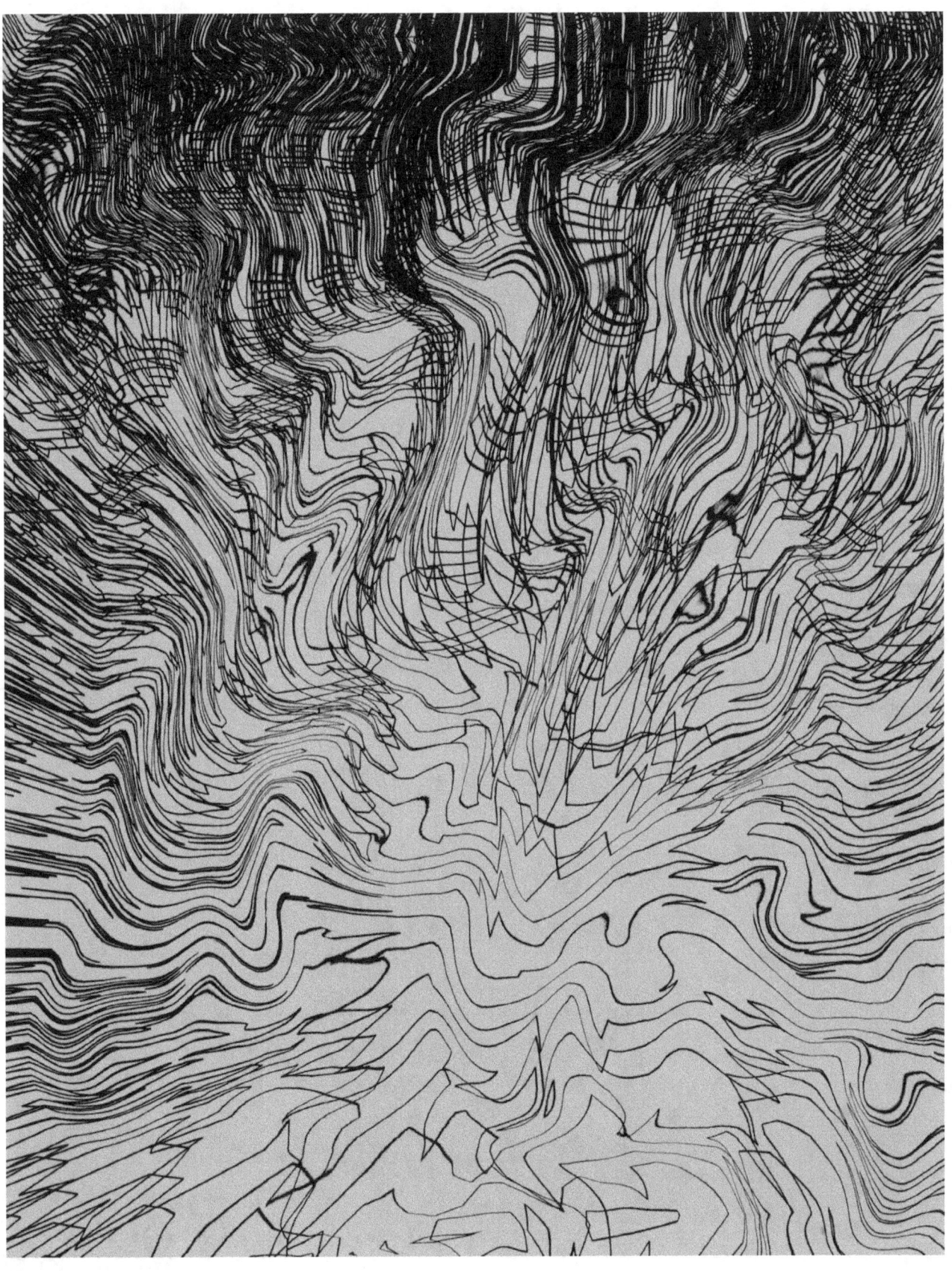

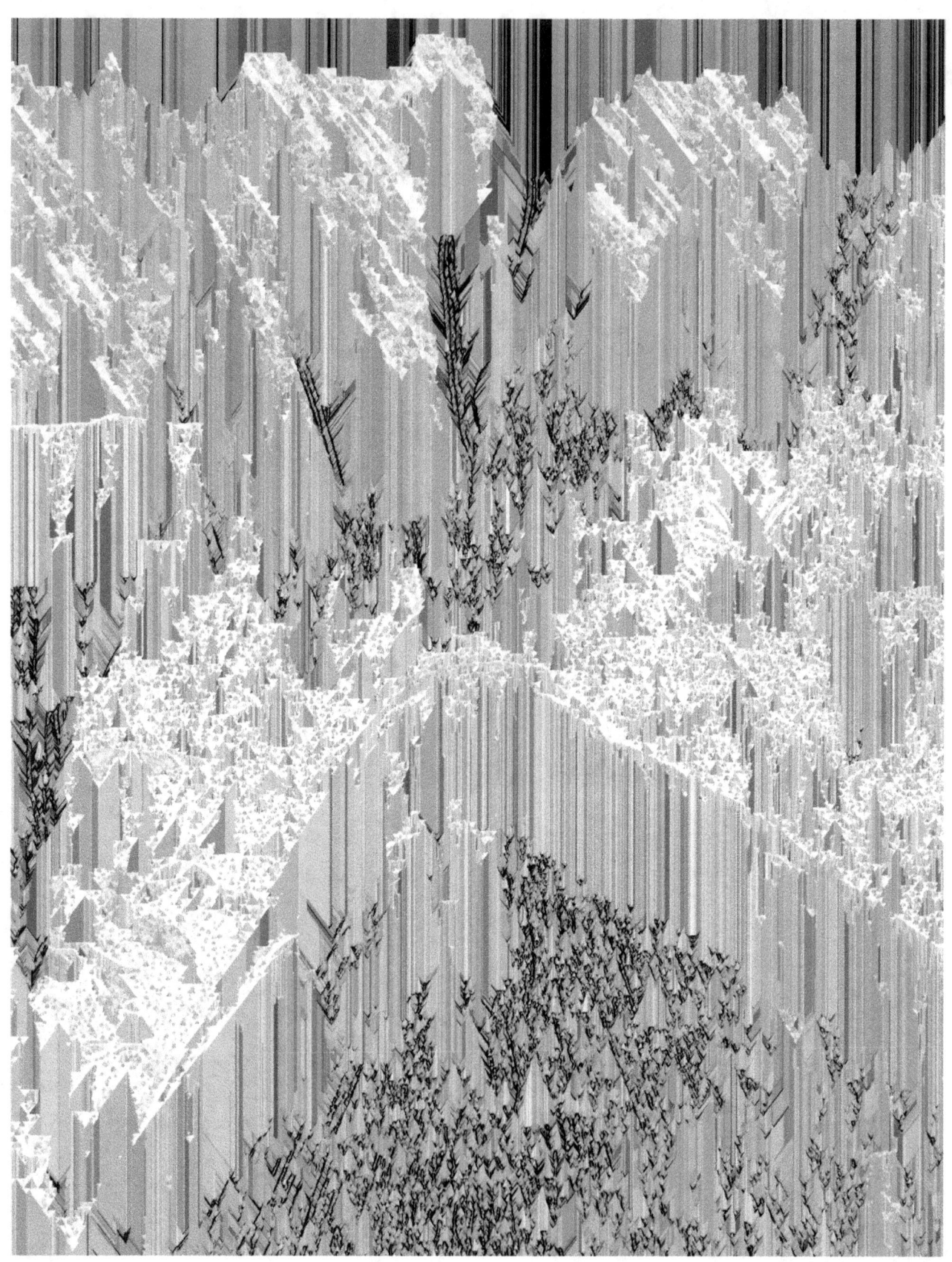

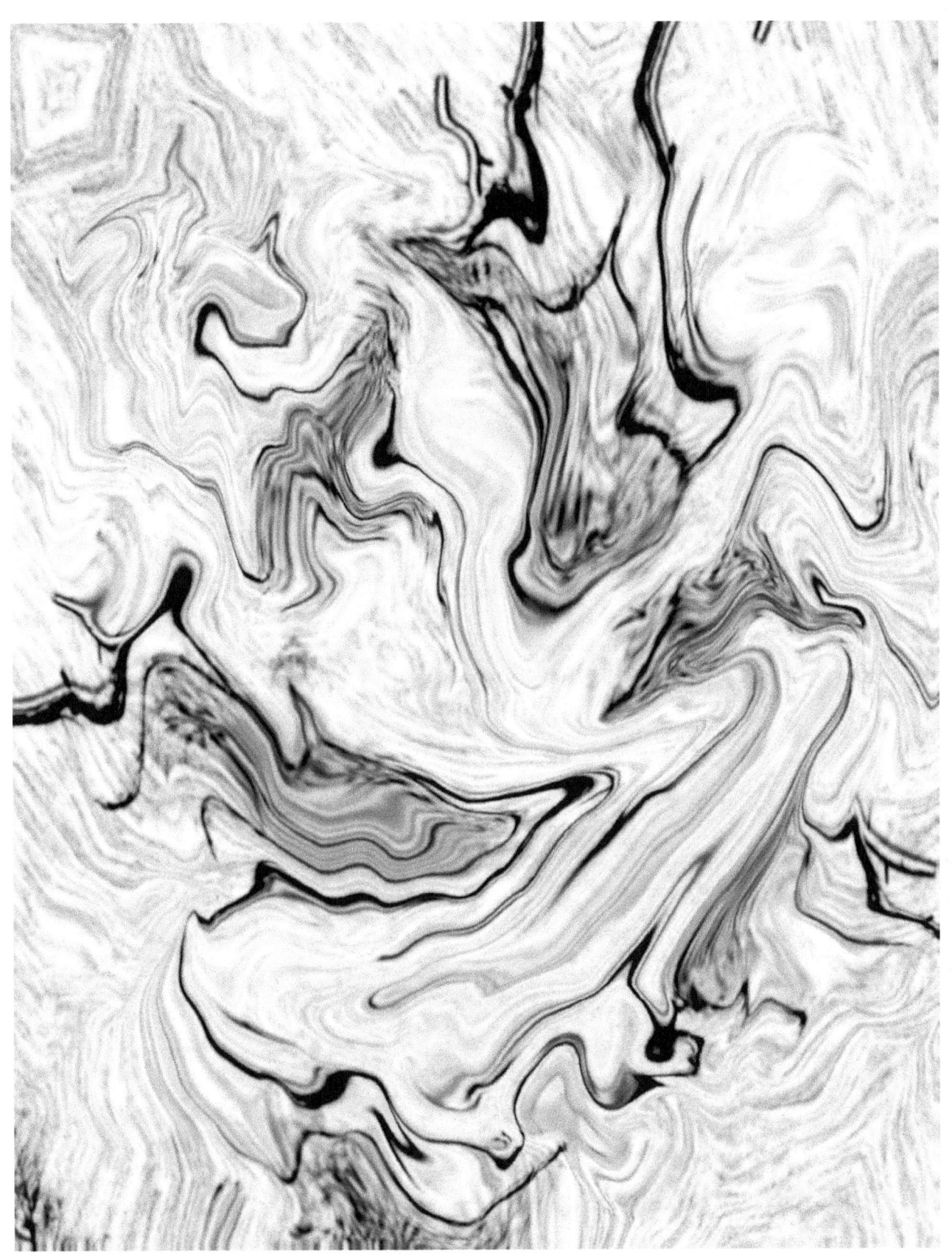

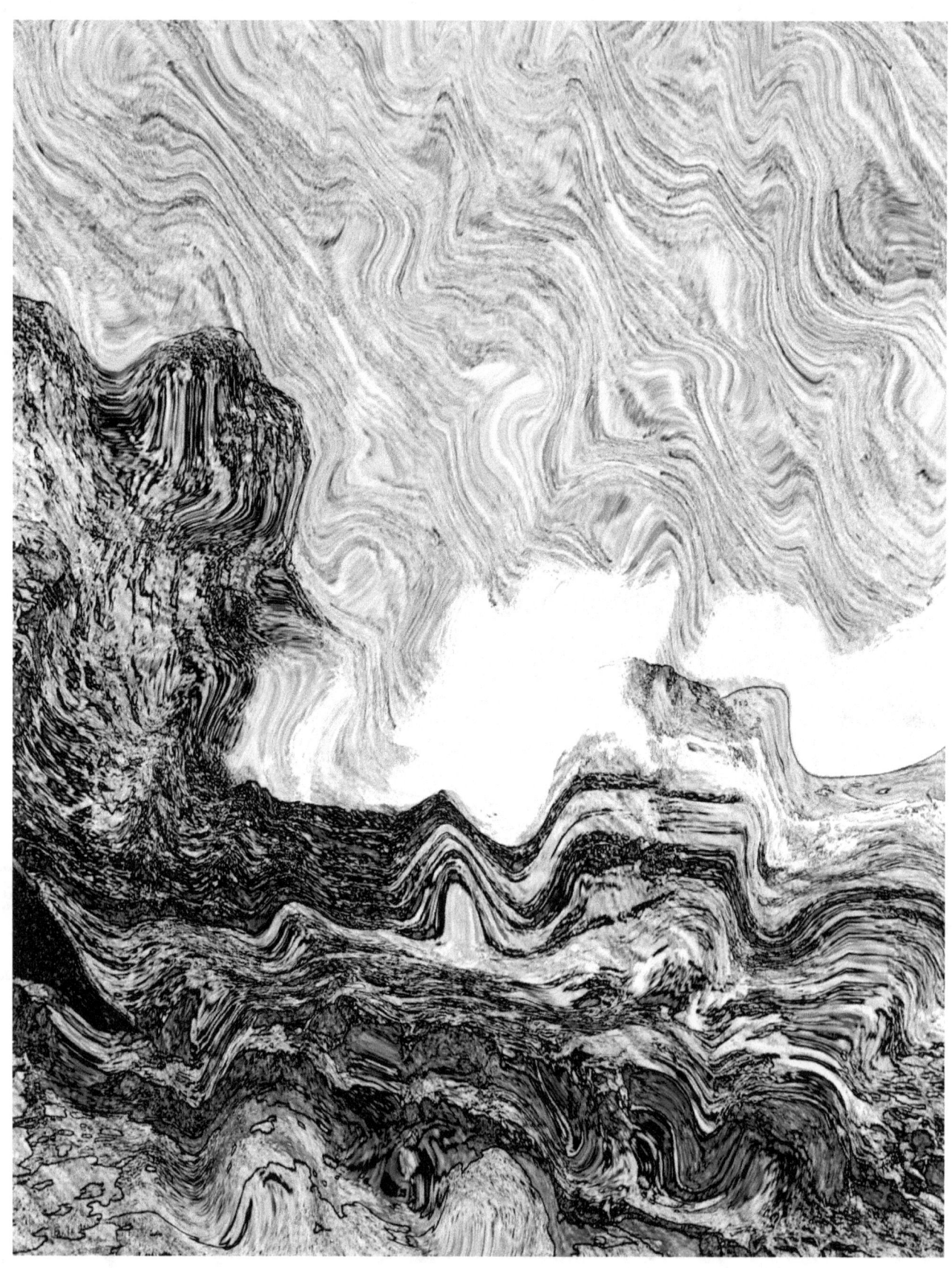

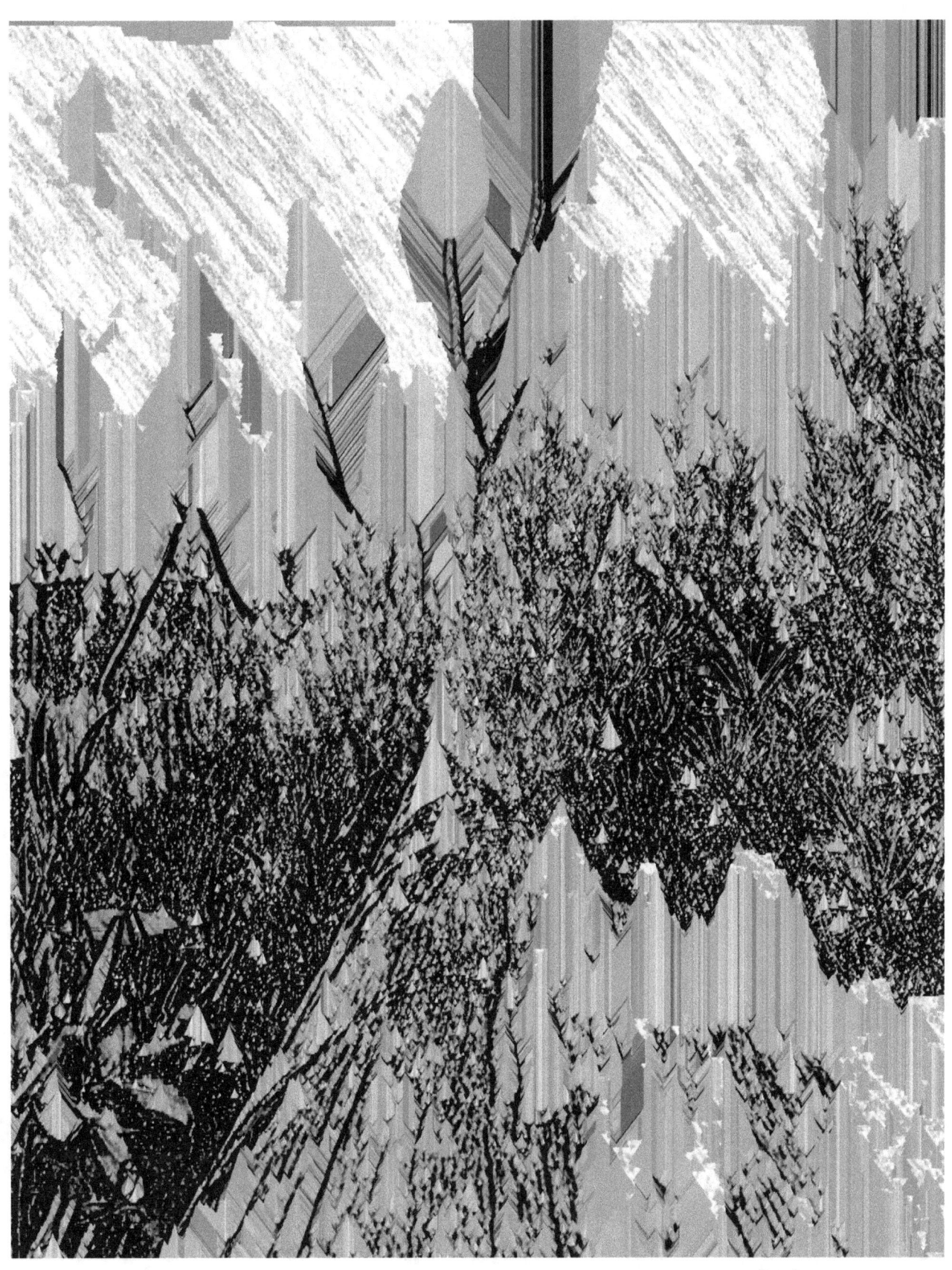

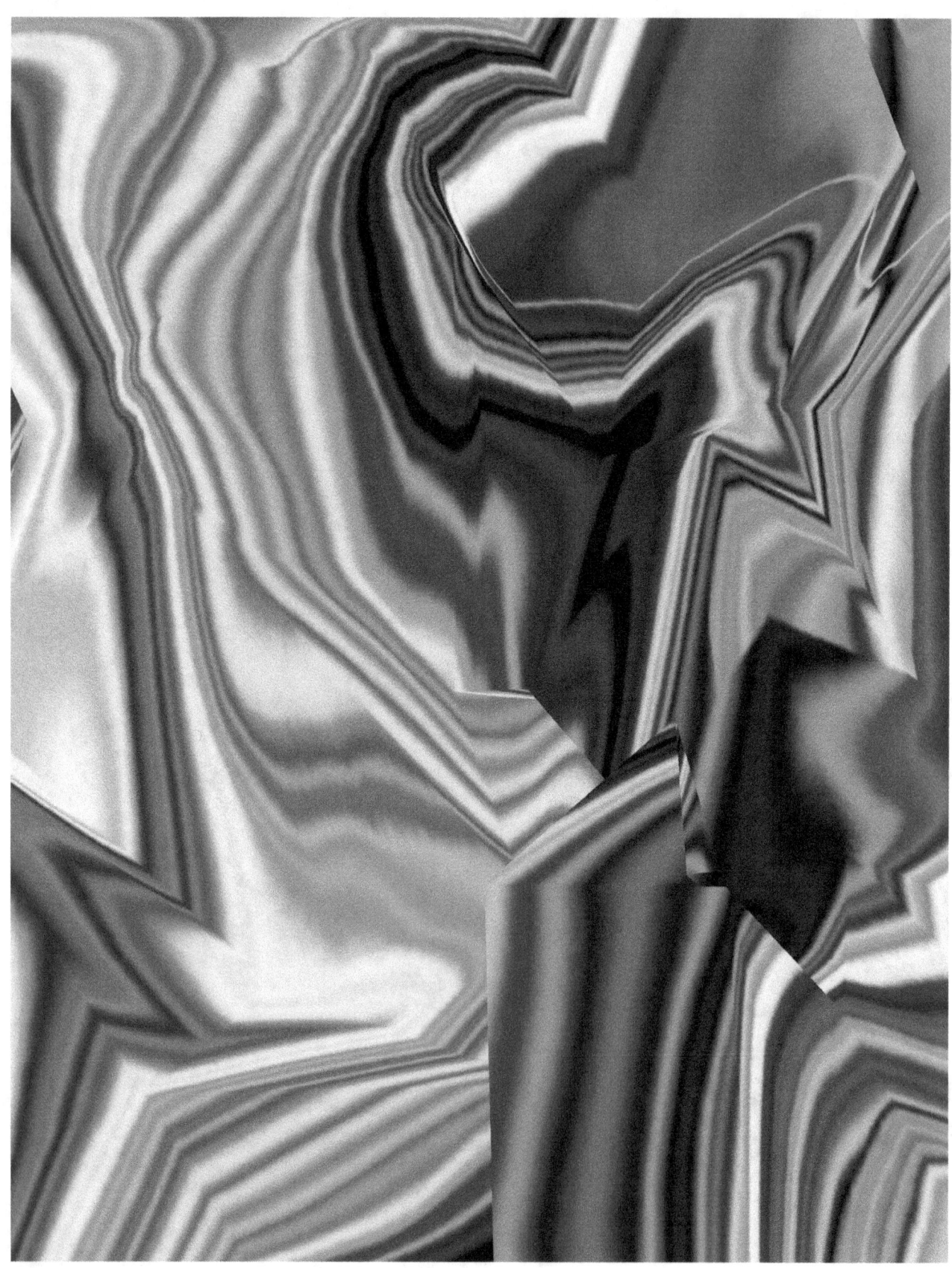

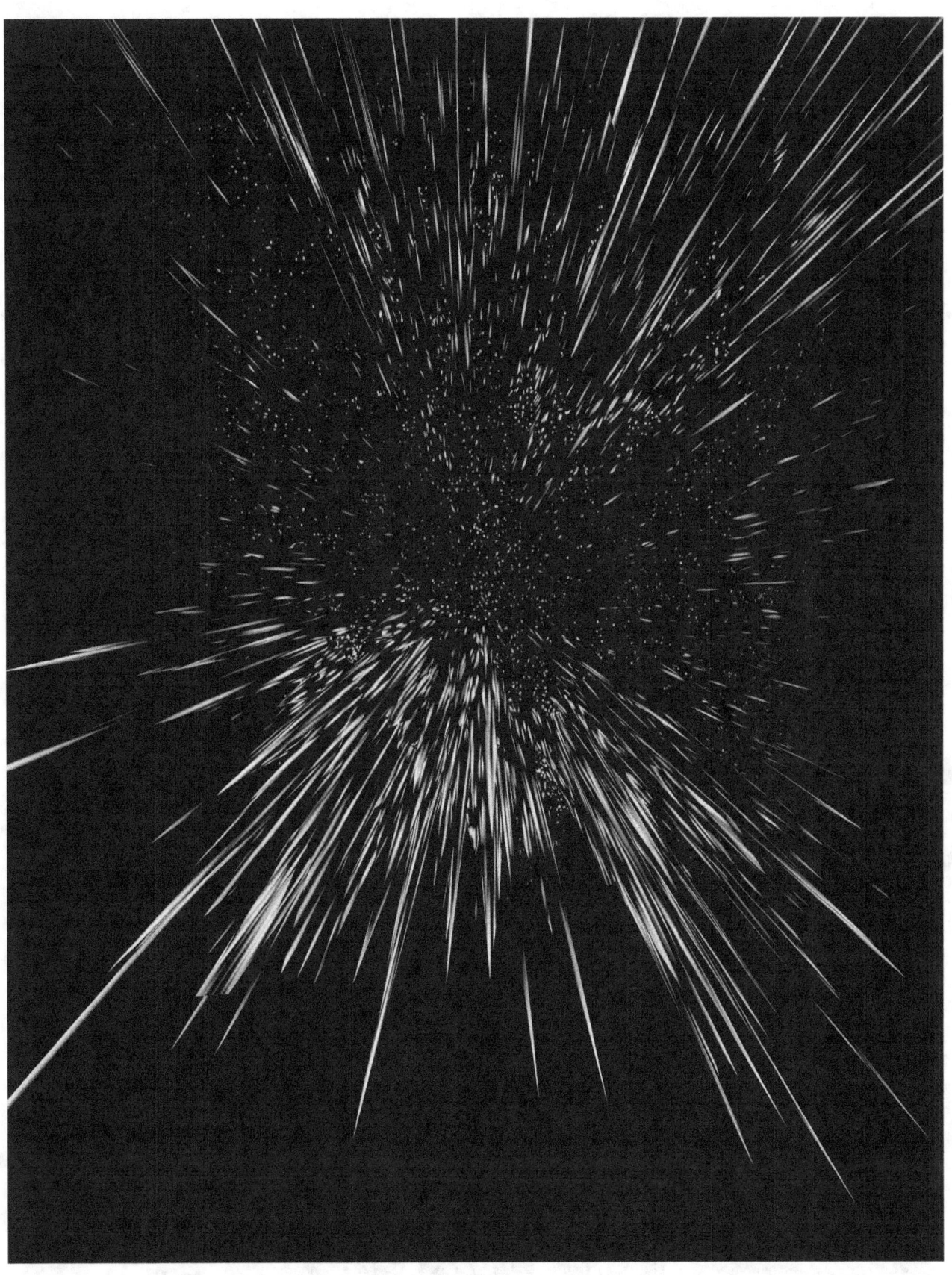

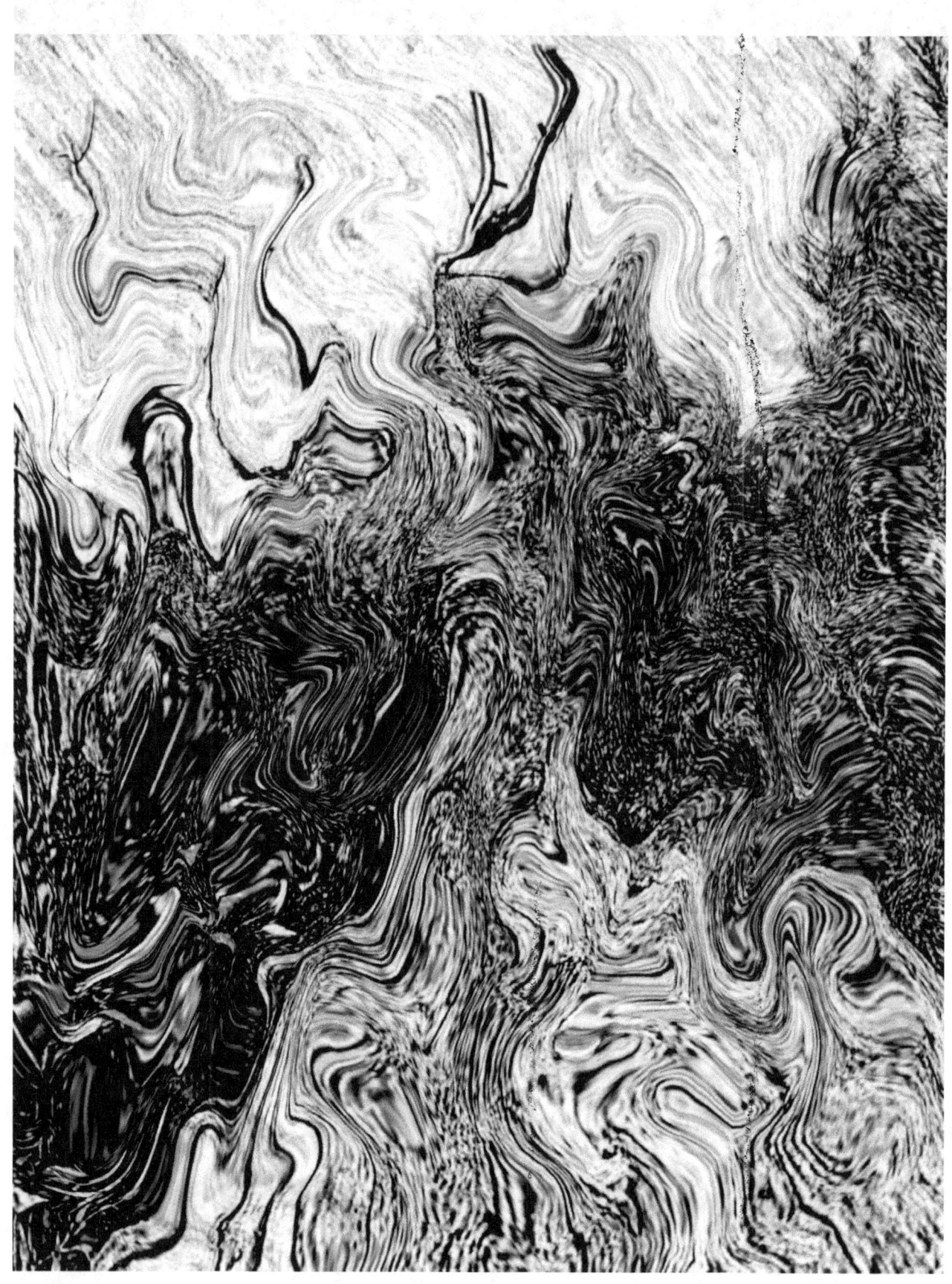